GREAT WARRIORS

PIRATES

KATE RIGGS

Published by Creative Paperbacks
P.O. Box 227, Mankato, Minnesota 56002
Creative Paperbacks is an imprint of The Creative Company
www.thecreativecompany.us

Design and production by Stephanie Blumenthal
Art direction by Rita Marshall
Printed by Corporate Graphics in the United States of America

Photographs by Alamy (Mary Evans Picture Library, North Wind Picture
Archives), Corbis (Bettmann, Blue Lantern Studio), Dreamstime, iStockphoto
Illustrations on back cover and p. 21 copyright © 2002 Roberto Innocenti

The Library of Congress has cataloged the hardcover edition as follows:
Riggs, Kate.
Pirates / by Kate Riggs.
p. cm. — (Great warriors)
Summary: A simple introduction to the roving warriors known as pirates, including their
history, lifestyle, weapons, and how they remain a part of today's culture by their continued existence.
Includes index.
ISBN 978-1-60818-002-8 (hardcover)
ISBN 978-0-89812-573-3 (pbk)
1. Pirates—Juvenile literature. I. Title. II. Series.
G535.R56 2011
910.4'5—dc22   2009048807
CPSIA: 040110 PO1137
First Edition
2 4 6 8 9 7 5 3 1

TABLE OF CONTENTS

WHO ARE PIRATES? 4

A PIRATE'S LIFE 9

FAMOUS PIRATES 18

GLOSSARY 24

READ MORE 24

INDEX 24

Sometimes people fight.

They fight for food. They fight for land. Or sometimes they fight for sport. Pirates are warriors who fight other people to steal treasures and ships.

A pirate's life was filled with fighting

Pirates have been fighting for 500 years. They have sailed ships on seas and oceans all over the world. Sailors, **criminals**, and anyone who wanted to get rich by stealing could be a pirate.

Pirates spent most of their time on ships

A LOT OF PIRATES
WORE AN EYE PATCH
BECAUSE THEY
INJURED AN EYE
DURING A FIGHT.

People did not train to be pirates. Some pirates already knew how to sail when they started. Some knew how to use weapons. Other pirates learned as they went along.

Pirates sometimes hid their treasure by burying it

Pirates have used many weapons. They used swords a long time ago. Then they used guns called muskets and pistols.

Pirates used any weapons they had to fight their enemies

AN EARLY PIRATE SWORD WAS CALLED A CUTLASS. IT WAS SHORT
AND THICK WITH A CURVED BLADE.

Pirates used ships to get where they needed to go. A good pirate ship could go faster than other ships. It could carry all the treasure the pirates stole. Ships also carried big guns like cannons.

A ship's flags let people know who owns the ship

THE SKULL AND CROSSBONES PICTURE ON A PIRATE FLAG IS CALLED THE "JOLLY ROGER."

Pirates went aboard other ships to steal from them. Sometimes they went on land and raided towns. Many people were afraid of pirates. So the pirates usually won the fights.

Pirates used small rowboats to get from their ships to land

MANY PIRATES LIKED TO VISIT THE TOWN OF PORT ROYAL IN THE **ISLAND** COUNTRY OF JAMAICA.

Pirates stayed at sea for weeks at a time. They worked on the ship. They played card games. Sometimes they got in trouble with the **captain**. Then they might have had to walk the plank!

A pirate who walked the plank then fell into the water

Blackbeard was a famous pirate in the 1700s. He **looted** many ships. But then British soldiers caught and killed him. Sir Henry Morgan was a pirate who worked for Great Britain. The **government** let him steal from other people.

Blackbeard got his name because of his long, dark beard

Most pirates stopped looting ships in the 1800s. That is when countries started catching more pirates. There are still pirates in the world today. But most people remember the pirates of old. They live on in movies and books!

Exciting stories about pirates can be found in many books

TODAY'S PIRATES DO NOT DIG FOR BURIED

TREASURE AS THEY ONCE DID.

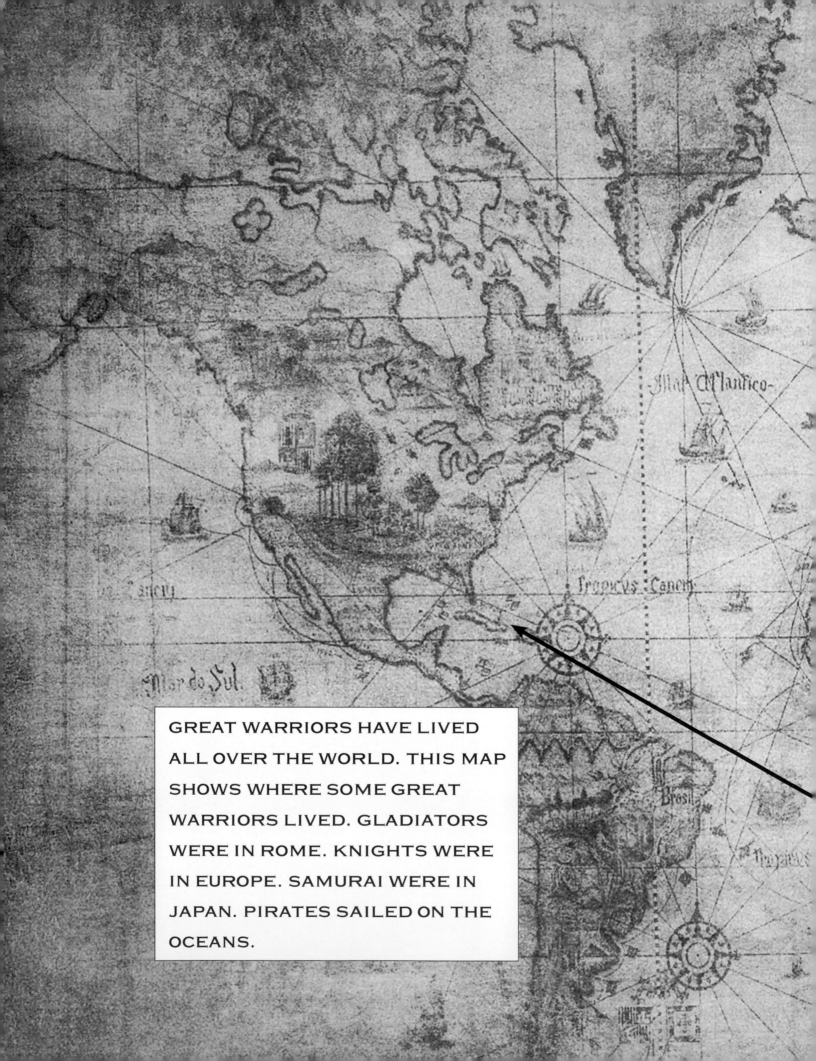

GREAT WARRIORS HAVE LIVED ALL OVER THE WORLD. THIS MAP SHOWS WHERE SOME GREAT WARRIORS LIVED. GLADIATORS WERE IN ROME. KNIGHTS WERE IN EUROPE. SAMURAI WERE IN JAPAN. PIRATES SAILED ON THE OCEANS.

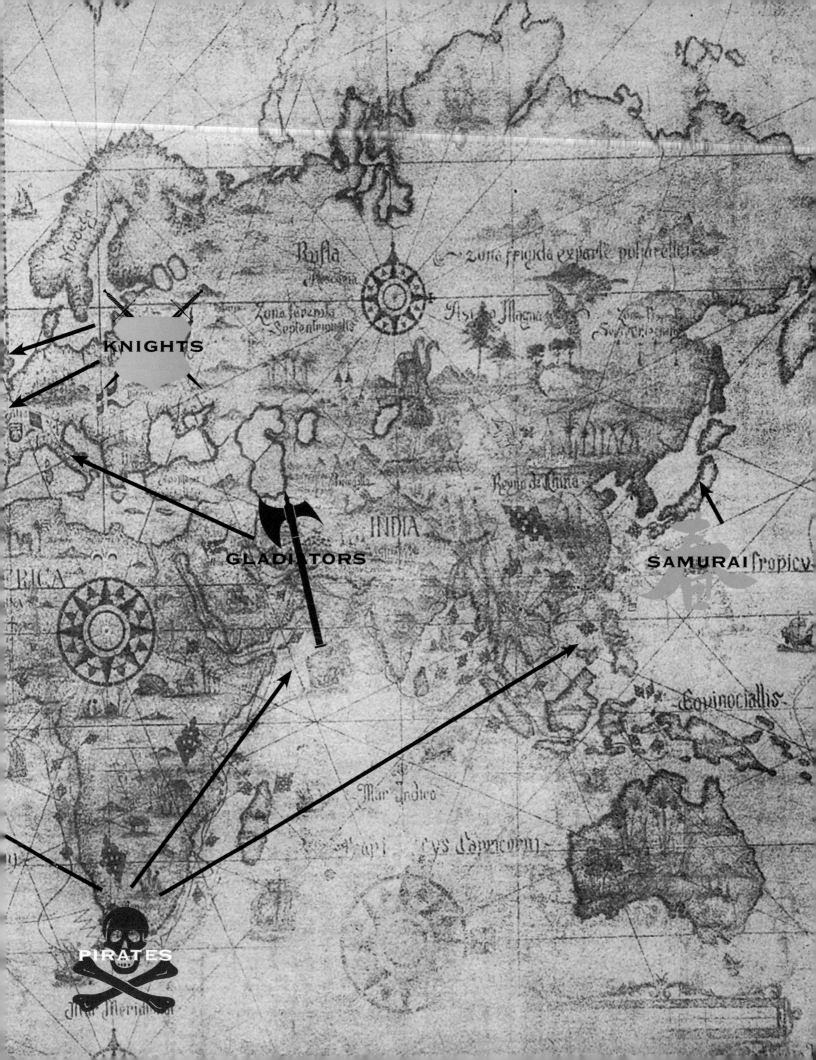

GLOSSARY

captain—the person in charge of a ship

criminals—people who break the law

government—a group that makes laws for the people of a state or country

island—a piece of land surrounded by water

looted—stole things from a place

READ MORE

Havercroft, Elizabeth. *A Year on a Pirate Ship*. Minneapolis: Millbrook Press, 2009.

Taplin, Sam. *The Usborne Official Pirate's Handbook*. London: Usborne, 2006.

INDEX

Blackbeard 18

captains 17, 18

Great Britain 18

lifestyle 7, 17

looting 18, 20

Morgan, Sir Henry 18

raids 14

sailing 6, 9

ships 4, 6, 12, 14, 17, 18, 20

training 9

treasures 4, 12

weapons 9, 10, 11, 12